Silver Seasons of Heartache

Naoko Fujimoto

Glass Lyre Press

Copyright © 2017 Naoko Fujimoto
Paperback ISBN: 978-1-941783-33-7

All rights reserved: except for the purpose of quoting brief passages for review, no part of this book may be reproduced or transmitted in any form or by any means, electronic or mechanical, including photocopying, recording, or by any information storage and retrieval system, without permission in writing from the publisher.

Cover art: Naoko Fujimoto
Design & layout: Steven Asmussen
Project Manager: Royce Hamel
Copyediting: Linda E. Kim

Glass Lyre Press, LLC
P.O. Box 2693
Glenview, IL 60025
www.GlassLyrePress.com

Contents

Acknowledgments	VII
Koi-Kokoro is One Step Before	1
The Explosion of Ivy Leaves	2
Lunch Time Atlas	3
Our Fourteenth Summer	4
Meadowsweet, Koi-kokoro	5
Leaf Blowers	8
Through an Indian Brick Town	9
Impossibly Long	10
Unlasted Improvisation	11
A Big Bowl of Beef Stew	12
Always Worry About Money	13
Draw the Light	14
Kapok-Tree	15
Electric Bills	16
Foreign/Gray	17
Today is Not October Seventh	18
Enough is Never	19
How Do I Love You Knowing I Will Eventually Lose You?	20
Kotobuki, Seven Pillow Cases	21
Helping My Father Dress	22

My Father's Ivory Die	23
How to Choke Myself in the Ugly Kitchen	24
Clay Cup from a Chai Stand	25
On the Blue Subway Line,	26
Spaghetti Harassment	27
Sakura, Sakura on the Radio	29
About the Author	31

for Aaron

Acknowledgments

Eternal thanks to these journals for publishing my original pieces: *Anti-, Big Scream, Cimarron Review, Cream City Review, Gargoyle Magazine, Juked, Natural Bridge, Pamplemousse, Pirene's Fountain, RHINO, Poemmemoirstory, Tangential Bird Piles,* and *The Cape Rock.*

Love to the Glass Lyre Press family, especially Ami Kaye, Royce Hamel, and Steven Asmussen.

Koi-Kokoro is One Step Before

being in love;

perhaps thinking of him in the edge of Wisconsin,
or in the corner of a corridor, wishing to have the courage
to ask him to walk by the river

among floating leaves
and stretched bat wings waiting for the rain to stop…

Through the torn umbrella,
I see them fly circles at four-thirty in the morning.

The nameless river is my *koi-kokoro,*

crossing cities and states to follow the lake— keep flowing,
don't tangle me— the reeds twine around my ankles.

Bring me scissors.

The Explosion of Ivy Leaves

Then, I hate.

I hate the explosion of ivy leaves.
Since puberty, I should have known better—
holding his hand under the dinner table

or whispering and finding a gray hair
behind his ear does not mean anything.

I smell the ice-beaded Michigan beach.

A wild animal hibernates
until its mating season.

Tweezers and pliers net my heart.

You know—I am actually happy.

I have an afghan to cover my feet.

On a couch, a black cat jumps.
She pries off her transparent nails on my naked knees.

With the noise of a reality television show,
I am smoldering young in the worst way,

never learned how to kiss in a winter rain.

Lunch Time Atlas

I say, "Take my hand,"

to climb up to the November clouds.
My flat shoes fell off but we must
leap to the cracked sky.

I look into his gray eyes and my mouth moves…

Beep,

the microwave in the lunch room.

He stands up and passes me down the stairs.
Sandwich crumbs dry out.

Today is the forty-seventh day, as speechless as yesterday.

I tune in a radio signal

and whisper,

"Do you like fried rice?"

Our Fourteenth Summer

The wind raises her black hair,
round beads roll down her neck.

Laundry flutters like young leaves,
never stops flapping between the breezes.

She bikes over endless country hills.

Come this way, short cut—she waves.

I follow her path, the sweet smell of her body.

That night,

we lie on a blanket and she asks me to touch her.
Her head rests on my shoulder.

She says, "Smile."

Her forefinger strokes my arm,
her lips rest on my clavicle.

I stand up

                and run down the cement porch steps.

Meadowsweet, Koi-kokoro

1.
Every summer, my grandfather wore
geta-slippers, so there was a gap
between his big toes and the others.

He kept telling me the same story. He sold
cloth and met a surveyor in China, 1944…

    Meadowsweet in a Japanese room.

        You turn in bed.

        I feel your warm feet
        in the cotton sheets.

        The warmth,   I wanted it before I was married.

2.
Koi-kokoro is love
written with a single stroke   like Japanese calligraphy.

3.
My grandmother sent me a poem
written by an Indian ink stick rubbed on an inkstone.

"I couldn't write my *koi-kokoro* to test the ink for color."

        You leave
        wet paint on my *koi-kokoro*.

Purple with yellow dots.

Covering colors with colors kills the art.

4.
The surveyor had bound feet
because he wore *geta*-slippers;
he was afraid of showing his Japanese feet in China.

When my grandfather died,
my grandmother dressed him in a mourning *kimono*.

but she couldn't put him in socks.　　　　His toes were too Japanese.

Since the funeral,
she wears his socks when she goes to bed.

She wants the warmth that I have.

5.
In my grandfather's diary,
the surveyor fell in love with a Chinese nurse.

She rubbed his foot
under the ink-blotting sky. The early

spring starts to arise after several strokes;

deep maple forests and meadowsweet in their mind…

6.
Crystal-clear February ice.   I shout,

"Don't ask me to make love when I write,"

then break every tea cup.

Leaf Blowers

"You will die shortly. Wear anything you want,"
I say to Grandmother and launder her black shawls.

A ghost swaddles her emerald broach.
Her shoes dim like young nails.

Piles of paper cut out Grandfather's face.

After his funeral, I lay under the piano.

Your fingers trill the keys;
leaf blowers reverberate my skull.

Hail bullets the soil.

If you die first, I have no idea—
for example, the cable television bill, its password,

and a complete set of crap.

More doorbell rings. A truck
drops off boxes.

Your unfertilized descendants carry them to the dumpster.

Through an Indian Brick Town

The best masala chai I ever had was with a Sikh.

Large earthen pots
lined brick walls around the hut.

He tilted one over and showed me inside.

Rain water never filled this dry town.

When he sipped tea,
he was quiet. The clay edge was rough

on our lips but melted the sweet sugar milk.
A strong ginger scent stayed with my palms.

I said, "What is all this rubble on the ground?"

"Step on it," and he crushed the empty cup.

A wild dog sniffed red shards.

I still held the cup on my knee.

A low fog curled my toes.
Fires crackled in kilns.

Impossibly Long

A big chunk of goat cheese sat on my plate.

My grandfather said,
"If you don't finish it, you cannot start dinner."

The asparagus was impossibly long on the golden fork.
Its strings got caught between my teeth.

The table was crowded with my parents,
cousins, grandmother, and baby sister—

My grandfather proudly told me,
"This restaurant only accepts ten Chinese people a day…"

But we are Japanese.

"It does not matter," he replied.

Roast beef sank in my stomach
on the way back to the hotel.

My frostbitten ears fell off on the eighth street. I kept
gazing at my grandfather's enamel shoes.

We walked

and walked on the cobblestone street

with a glimpse of Paris gray,
living under foreign skin.

Unlasted Improvisation

A swallow cuts the mist with its face,
wings in the chilled beer.

The bass clef howls and my hair rises against gravity;

smoke whirls around my head—
flashing like needles on the black keys.

I blast

fireworks of silvery trills and fly over amber hills.

Scimitar nails tick triplet beats.
My high heels trample; crescendo tempo leaps…

You tap your pencil on a desk and say,

"How do we split this bill?"

A Big Bowl of Beef Stew

Coffee tightened my throat—*how much I missed him*,
but I could not say it, instead I said—

what I said, I do not remember.

A big bowl of beef stew steamed.
He added pepper to every spoonful.

                We picked up ginkgo and maple leaves

and I wanted him to say,
"See you at dinner on Wednesday night."

The autumn was not so lonely, nor long of nights.

Past midnight, from the deepest forest,
a deer walked on weathered leaves.

Always Worry About Money

My grandmother wears a faded
apron and eats

pickled Japanese radishes,

grains of rice,

oranges,

but she shrinks

like a mummified Egyptian cat.

How much is my kidney?

She turns over sales slips
with her worm-hand;

her parchment fingers and

she holds a cup of tea.

There is a sugar jar—

unexpired lumps linger
from a Chinese cabinet;

conceal my tongue.

Ash falls from her cremation;
sunlight bakes the blind.

Draw the Light

His breath is quiet—
               waiting to catch the last lightning bug.

Sunlight sweeps the room and windows.

"Your thighs are beautiful,"
he says holding a brush and sketching my body.

"That is enough color to draw the light," he says without looking at me.

The only brown is on the desk...

He lives in a small house.

Dewdrops drip down its thatch roof,
my white sandals, stained from the summer dirt,

soak his sleeves overnight.

Kapok-Tree

You say, "Vinegar spray kills them."

Caterpillars crawl through shrubs— skeleton stems shake.

When they chew the last leaf,
they die with their heads up and turn black

like pumice stones.

I turn on the porch lamp. A butterfly dives
between the kapok-tree and its intense belts of cobwebs.

It lays an egg behind each leaf.

                A scythe slices the night sky and Jupiter appears.

The gas swirls everything around it.
You say, "Deadly dangerous."

Chrysalises thread a screen door.
When I shut it, some fell.

Electric Bills
after the tsunami on 3/11/2011

You are part of a white

field under wet sweaters. A tin
box is tangled in your hair. In the box,

there are electric

bills that say, *Have a bright day!* If
it is your spiritual

message, I want to turn off the light.

I need a chair that my body
drops into so I can dream about the smell of

your neck.

Somebody yells, *Is anyone alive?*

…no, it snows here and it is difficult to close my eyes.

Foreign/Gray
after the tsunami on 3/11/2011

Because I'm from Fukushima, I say, I'm not / radioactive, and eat / seaweed salad from a bowl. You / hold my hands as we share these long / silences. Because / I'm a Buddhist, I recite, Namu-amida-butsu, at noon / over lunch, and very late at night. But I don't pray for the Japanese. I pray / for myself because I crave / a word. I want it to avalanche into my eyes / like a kaleidoscope for the dead, but the sky / glares as usual because I'm so / often lost in this foreign / grey. I take my two fingers and push / them into my breasts. I say, If I / die with cancer, for example? You rub / my left breast. My brown / nipples are so cold at 2:30 A.M.

*Namu-amida-butsu is a phrase from Buddhist prayer.

Today is Not October Seventh

If today is not October Seventh,
she is not standing over the bridge.

White scattering stars cover street lamps.
Spots are orange in my foot prints.

I think of her more than she thinks of me.
Don't let the lamps go out.

I am too scared to sleep and my feet are cold.
Ghostly clouds surround my head and whisper Bach's song.

I still do not know why I couldn't. I couldn't say,

"Touch me"—

Her body weighs almost nothing in the rippling river.

Enough is Never

"I will take the trash out," he says.
The door closes in a small house.

Our hearts, like rhubarbs,
liquidate in a garbage disposal.

Magpies bring pieces from the glass company
adding more stones to the riverbank.

I glue my deodorant in his cabinet
because enough is never enough.

Hair upholsters my eyes on his sheets.
"Orange toenails," he says.

I slip my feet under his thighs.

We hear her lively laugh—
a neighborhood girl raises her sunglasses

with freckles on her clavicles,
her white dress flares.

How Do I Love You Knowing I Will Eventually Lose You?
after a missing poet on a Japanese island— Kuchinoerabu-jima

While a poet kept walking   walking toward the east
    and fell off a cliff,

you held my hand   *Will you marry me?*
    and I said, Yes

because I thought—

you were not the kind of guy who would die before me

    and if you did,
        my life wouldn't be peculiar

(I would make love to your groomsman

in our bed on the day

        after your funeral).

Crickets laid eggs in the still of the night.

The Japanese sky was like dark
    cerulean stone   the poet

closed his eyes to inhale the pinewoods—

    You sang Wagner
        and I threw away a white baneberry.

Kotobuki, Seven Pillow Cases

Twelve days after we purchased
a queen size bed, my mother

cries on the phone asking,
"Do you have pillow cases?"

She means seven pillow cases: pink
silk, green satin, white cotton...

Under the sheets, I think of her. Naked
pillows were knocked to the floor Thursday afternoon.

"There is no *kotobuki* in your marriage,"
My mother still cries. She wanted to wrap

the pillow cases in thin white
paper and *kotobuki*: the wedding

symbols of gold
wires made of turtles & cranes; to keep

her busy enough to forget;
I'm leaving her Japanese home.

"Mrs. Nakajima showed her pillow cases..."
Her daughter married a Nagoya-

born pharmacist. We went to the same
elementary school but I didn't jump.

---

* *Kotobuki* means happiness and congratulations (blessing) from immediate family and friends.

Helping My Father Dress

His left hand first, then his elbow—
he does not remember where his head goes.

My nephew brings his small shirt.
His arms are up high and quickly leave to his apple juice.

My father mumbles, "Is he your son?"

His unfocused eyes
gaze at the floor, holding the wrong sock.

I tap his right thigh twice to raise his foot.

He asks me to turn on his record,
Bach's Cantatas—

He conducts the symphony and says,

"Why was I not invited to your wedding?"

My Father's Ivory Die

#3: additional / seizures after his brain / surgery, #5: broken / front teeth from diabetes… / my father throws / his ivory die on the floor / I say, #4: "You may die within three / years, you know?" / he flaps /yesterday's newspaper #2: because his tears / blur out an article about a comet —even after a star / dies, #6: it may linger as a white / dwarf— I hear / the clatter of dishes and silverware #1: I push / his wheelchair / the die rolls into a corner of the dining room / silken layers of stardust cover it / he scoops / egg-drop soup into his mouth.

How to Choke Myself in the Ugly Kitchen

When I stumbled on the kitchen floor,
I actually believed in a counterclockwise wonderland—

colorful macaroons and a mouthful of sherbet. Dried

skin flaked in my long hair. It covered
my lineless back. I saw some moles.

Then he called me, *Sweetie*—

without kissing my forehead.

Once he drilled a hole and hung a phone from the 1970s,
and painted the wall a puke yellow.

I shoveled a spoonful of instant coffee into my mouth.

There is

an extra season of endless fields...
The postcard fell from the refrigerator.

Sweetie, he called me from behind a leather couch.

The TV remote is lonely on the carpet.

I wiped my hands with a paper towel and said, *I am here.*

Clay Cup from a Chai Stand

This particular one is from a chai stand in India.
Unopened envelopes are scattered underneath it.

A man dusted off clay cups with his fingers.
He said, "Three thousand dollars in a year."

I spend the same amount in a month. You know—
rent is higher here and bills are as frightening as

the unpasteurized milk in his tin can. He scooped

some water and said,
"I have four daughters, a wife, and a sick mother."

I replied, "My husband has no job."

The man scraped

spice onto the rim of the boiling pot. The burnt
smell reminded me of his front teeth. He smiled,

We are living in dream.

Saffron flowers bloomed on the street. Coconuts
and bright colors for *Ganesha*—let's worship,

so his daughters find a way to school
and we never starve eating cauliflower… Cut off

my head

and line it with the coconuts if the god is to hear us.

Don't explain how it works. I am just dealing with this reality.

On the Blue Subway Line,

St. Pachomius wiped windows and scraped chewing gum.
He sprayed seats;
the hibiscus ocean scent filled the dark and musty inside.

Nobody kneeled down toward the saint,
but they said, "Now, the saint is taking over our jobs."

They gazed at him—murderous in a way—eyes upon eyes.
Their fists beat the rims of their seats.

"Where is my job," the banging gets louder.
"How can I feed my family," they kicked the backs of the seats.

They marched around the Saint and kept screaming,
"Where is my miracle, where is my miracle?"

The hibiscus scent was gone, but human sweat remained.

Seconds later, they already forget St. Pachomius was here.
They quickly left from the train to where they belong.

Spaghetti Harassment

It is a dreadful poem in the Year of Spaghetti

in *Nagoya,*

because there is no spaghetti
to boil at *Tsurumae* Station. The *kishimen*

there is like eternally boiled fettuccine

as white as

a Pomeranian. It yaps in a stainless pot,
but there is no promise to be drained into a strainer.

Instead, it is in miso soup,
drowning with an uncooked egg yolk.
"Listen. *Kishimen* is unreliable,"
he says, and pushes my back to the rail track.

The official cause of death is an apparent suicide—

The truth is the train is three million pounds of dough.
It extrudes from eighty-three tiny holes

and strangles my tongue.

The wet spaghetti strands flood from the phone receiver.

"This is a life-size board game. Roll two dice," he grins.

His one-way ticket blazes away.

In my shadow, I see
the perfect shape of my nipples when I fall into the railway.

I cannot die until I add fried shrimp to the bowl of *kishimen*,

soft, and a little bit salty,

a taste of my young adult years.

Sakura, Sakura on the Radio

Guitarists played an old Japanese folk song.
Cherry blossoms shut for a long time,

sudden   gray-pink petals burst; yellow stamens

covered the streets when I walked through at *Tokugawa* Park.
I picked up the blossoms

and pressed them in telephone books
before being ruined by rain-drops—

I was careful,

careful to touch these now transparent
beautiful existences. I handed the best to my mother…

A couple of snowflakes landed
on the windshield. The lyric, I forgot.

About the Author

Naoko Fujimoto was born and raised in Nagoya, Japan. She was an exchange student and received a B.A. and M.A. from Indiana University South Bend. Her first chapbook, *Home, No Home*, won the annual Oro Fino Chapbook Competition by Educe Press. Currently she is working on her graphic poetry collection, which will be published by Tupelo Press. Her progress can be seen at her blog: http://naokofujimoto.blogspot.com.

Glass Lyre Press

exceptional works to replenish the spirit

Glass Lyre Press is an independent literary publisher interested in technically accomplished, stylistically distinct, and original work. Glass Lyre seeks diverse writers that possess a dynamic aesthetic and an ability to emotionally and intellectually engage a wide audience of readers.

Glass Lyre's vision is to connect the world through language and art. We hope to expand the scope of poetry and short fiction for the general reader through exceptionally well-written books, which evoke emotion, provide insight, and resonate with the human spirit.

Poetry Collections
Poetry Chapbooks
Select Short & Flash Fiction
Anthologies

www.GlassLyrePress.com